Summary

The 109th and 110th Congresses considered, but did not enact, comprehensive immigration reform legislation that included large-scale legalization programs for unauthorized aliens. In the aftermath of these unsuccessful efforts, some interested parties have urged the President and Congress to pursue more limited legislation to address the status of unauthorized alien students. Such legislation is commonly referred to as the "DREAM Act."

Unauthorized aliens in the United States are able to receive free public education through high school. They may experience difficulty obtaining higher education, however, for several reasons. Among these reasons is a provision enacted in 1996 that prohibits states from granting unauthorized aliens certain postsecondary educational benefits on the basis of state residence, unless equal benefits are made available to all U.S. citizens. This prohibition is commonly understood to apply to the granting of "in-state" residency status for tuition purposes. Unauthorized alien students also are not eligible for federal student financial aid. More broadly, as unauthorized aliens, they are not legally allowed to work and are subject to being removed from the country.

Multiple DREAM Act bills have been introduced in recent Congresses to address the unauthorized student population. Most have proposed a two-prong approach of repealing the 1996 provision and enabling some unauthorized alien students to become U.S. legal permanent residents (LPRs) through an immigration procedure known as *cancellation of removal*. While there are other options for dealing with this population, this report deals exclusively with the DREAM Act approach in light of the considerable congressional interest in it.

In the 111th Congress, the House approved DREAM Act language as part of an unrelated bill, the Removal Clarification Act of 2010. However, the Senate failed, on a 55-41 vote, to invoke cloture on a motion to agree to the House-passed DREAM Act amendment and the bill died at the end of the Congress. The House-approved language differed in key respects from earlier versions of the DREAM Act.

Bills to legalize the status of unauthorized alien students (S. 952, H.R. 1842, H.R. 3823) have again been introduced in the 112th Congress. It is unclear, however, whether any of these measures will be considered.

On June 15, 2012, the Obama Administration announced that certain individuals who were brought to the United States as children and meet other criteria would be considered for relief from removal. Under a memorandum issued by Secretary of Homeland Security Janet Napolitano on that date, these individuals would be eligible for deferred action for two years, subject to renewal, and could apply for employment authorization.

Contents

Appendixes

Contacts

RECENT DEVELOPMENTS

On June 15, 2012, the Obama Administration announced that certain individuals who were brought to the United States as children and meet other criteria would be considered for relief from removal. Under the memorandum, issued by Secretary of Homeland Security Janet Napolitano, these individuals would be eligible for deferred action[1] for two years, subject to renewal, and could apply for employment authorization.[2] The eligibility criteria for deferred action under the June 15, 2012, memorandum are (1) under age 16 at time of entry into the United States; (2) continuous residence in the United States for a least five years immediately preceding the date of the memorandum; (3) in school, graduated from high school or obtained general education development certificate, or honorably discharged from the Armed Forces; (4) not convicted of a felony offense, a significant misdemeanor offense, or multiple misdemeanor offenses, and not otherwise a threat to national security or public safety; and (5) age 30 or below. These eligibility criteria are similar to those included in DREAM Act bills discussed below. The deferred action process set forth in the June 15, 2012, memorandum, however, would not grant eligible individuals a legal immigration status.[3]

Introduction

While prospects for comprehensive immigration reform—which encompasses highly controversial proposals for legalization of unauthorized (illegal) aliens—may have dimmed in recent years, narrower proposals to enable unauthorized alien students to legalize their status have received attention. While still controversial, such proposals for legalization of aliens who were brought, as children, to live in the United States by their parents or other adults have enjoyed a broad base of support in recent Congresses.

While living in the United States, unauthorized alien children are able to receive free public education through high school.[4] Many unauthorized immigrants who graduate from high school and want to attend college, however, face various obstacles. Among them, a provision enacted in

---

[1] Deferred action is "a discretionary determination to defer removal action of an individual as an act of prosecutorial discretion." U.S. Department of Homeland Security, "Secretary Napolitano Announces Deferred Action Process for Young People Who Are Low Enforcement Priorities," http://www.dhs.gov/files/enforcement/deferred-action-process-for-young-people-who-are-low-enforcement-priorities.shtm. For additional information on prosecutorial discretion and deferred action, see Testimony of Ruth Ellen Wasem, Congressional Research Service, at U.S. Congress, House Committee on Homeland Security, Subcommittee on Border and Maritime Security, *Does Administrative Amnesty Harm our Efforts to Gain and Maintain Operational Control of the Border?*, hearing, 112th Congress, 1st sess., October 4, 2011, http://homeland.house.gov/sites/homeland.house.gov/files/Testimony%20Wasem.pdf.

[2] U.S. Department of Homeland Security, Memorandum to David V. Aguilar, Acting Commissioner, U.S. Customs and Border Protection, Alejandro Mayorkas, Director, U.S. Citizenship and Immigration Services, John Morton, Director, U.S. Immigration and Customs Enforcement, from Janet Napolitano, Secretary of Homeland Security, *Exercising Prosecutorial Discretion with Respect to Individuals Who Came to the United States as Children*, June 15, 2012, http://www.dhs.gov/xlibrary/assets/s1-exercising-prosecutorial-discretion-individuals-who-came-to-us-as-children.pdf.

[3] The memorandum states: "This memorandum confers no substantive right, immigration status or pathway to citizenship. Only the Congress, acting through its legislative authority, can confer these rights. It remains for the executive branch, however, to set forth policy for the exercise of discretion within the framework of the existing law." Ibid., p. 3.

[4] For a discussion of the legal basis for the provision of free public education, see CRS Report RS22500, *Unauthorized Alien Students, Higher Education, and In-State Tuition Rates A Legal Analysis*, by Jody Feder.

1996 as part of the Illegal Immigration Reform and Immigrant Responsibility Act (IIRIRA)[5] discourages states and localities from granting unauthorized aliens certain "postsecondary education benefits." More broadly, as unauthorized aliens, they are unable to work legally and are subject to removal from the United States.[6]

Multiple bills have been introduced in recent Congresses to provide relief to unauthorized alien students. These bills have often been entitled the Development, Relief, and Education for Alien Minors Act, or the DREAM Act. In this report, however, following common usage, the term DREAM Act is used to refer to similar bills to provide relief to unauthorized alien students whether or not they carry that name.

Prior to the 111th Congress, DREAM Act bills generally proposed to repeal the 1996 provision and to enable certain unauthorized alien students to adjust to legal permanent resident (LPR) status. In the 111th Congress, in December 2010, the House approved a different type of DREAM Act measure as part of an unrelated bill, the Removal Clarification Act of 2010 (H.R. 5281). Unlike earlier DREAM Act bills, the DREAM Act language in H.R. 5281 (which was the same as in stand-alone H.R. 6497) did not include a repeal of the 1996 provision and proposed to grant eligible individuals an interim legal status prior to enabling them to adjust to LPR status. The Senate failed, on a 55-41 vote, to invoke cloture on a motion to agree to the House-passed DREAM Act amendment, and H.R. 5281 died at the end of the Congress.

Bills to legalize the status of unauthorized alien students (S. 952, H.R. 1842, H.R. 3823) have again been introduced in the 112th Congress. S. 952 and H.R. 1842 take a step back from some of the revisions incorporated in the DREAM Act measure approved by the House in the 111th Congress and include some more traditional DREAM Act provisions. By contrast, H.R. 3823 includes many of the same provisions as the House-approved measure, but it is more restrictive in some respects. The outlook for the consideration or enactment of these or any other DREAM Act bills, however, is unclear.

Estimates of Potential DREAM Act Beneficiaries

As discussed below, DREAM Act bills introduced in recent Congresses would enable certain unauthorized alien students to obtain LPR status in the United States, in the case of most bills through a two-stage process. Requirements to obtain conditional status (stage 1) typically include residence of at least five years in the United States and a high school diploma (or the equivalent) or admission to an institution of higher education in the United States. Requirements to become a full-fledged LPR (stage 2) typically include acquisition of a degree from an institution of higher education in the United States, completion of at least two years in a bachelor's or higher degree program, or service in the uniformed services for at least two years.

In 2010, using data from the March 2006, March 2007, and March 2008 CPS and other sources, the Migration Policy Institute (MPI) published estimates of the population potentially eligible for

---

[5] IIRIRA is Division C of P.L. 104-208, September 30, 1996.

[6] Unauthorized alien students are distinct from a group commonly referred to as foreign students. Like unauthorized alien students, foreign students are foreign nationals. Unlike unauthorized alien students, however, foreign students enter the United States legally on nonimmigrant (temporary) visas in order to study at U.S. institutions.

legal status under S. 729, a Senate DREAM Act bill introduced in the 111th Congress.[7] This bill would have established a two-stage process for unauthorized alien students to obtain LPR status. As detailed below,[8] aliens who met specified age, physical presence, educational, and other requirements could have first applied for conditional LPR status. After meeting additional requirements, including two years of either college or service in the uniformed services, they could have applied to have the condition on their status removed and become full-fledged LPRs.

According to the MPI analysis, if this DREAM Act bill had been enacted, about 2.150 million individuals could have attempted to become LPRs under its provisions. This total included estimates of individuals who, on the date of enactment, would already have met the substantive requirements under the bill for conditional status (or for both conditional status and the removal of the condition), as well as estimates of individuals who, on the date of enactment, would have met some, but not all, of the requirements for conditional status. About 43% (934,000) of the estimated 2.150 million potential beneficiaries were children under age 18 in elementary or secondary school. The MPI report also included an estimate of the number of individuals who would likely have obtained LPR status under S. 729, if it had been enacted:

> If future behavior mirrors past trends, we project that approximately 38 percent [of the 2.1 million]—or 825,000—of the potential beneficiaries would actually achieve lawful permanent status under the legislation.[9]

As part of a 2010 analysis of the costs and likely impact of DREAM Act legislation before the 111th Congress, the Center for Immigration Studies (CIS) similarly estimated the number of potential DREAM Act beneficiaries using 2009 and 2010 CPS data.[10] Although CIS did not identify the bills at issue in its analysis, the bill requirements mentioned matched those in S. 729, as described above, and S. 3827, a similar bill introduced in the 111th Congress.[11] CIS estimated that there were some 1.998 million unauthorized aliens who would have met the residency and age requirements under the DREAM Act legislation, including 859,000 children under age 18. Of the 1.998 million potential beneficiaries, CIS estimated that 1.426 million individuals would have met the high school graduation, or equivalent, requirement for conditional LPR status (either on the date of enactment or at a later date). CIS, however, did not provide an estimate of the number of individuals who likely would have obtained LPR status under the DREAM Act.

Higher Education Benefits and Immigration Status

Under federal law, unauthorized aliens are neither entitled to nor prohibited from admission to postsecondary educational institutions in the United States. State laws vary and may prohibit enrollment in public postsecondary institutions. To gain entrance to available institutions, unauthorized aliens must meet the same requirements as any other student, which vary depending on the institution and may include possessing a high school diploma, passing entrance exams, and

---

[7] Jeanne Batalova and Margie McHugh, *DREAM vs. Reality An Analysis of Potential DREAM Act Beneficiaries*, Migration Policy Institute, July 2010, http://www.migrationpolicy.org (hereinafter cited as MPI, *DREAM vs. Reality*).

[8] See description of S. 729 in "Legislation in the 111th Congress" in **Appendix**.

[9] MPI, *DREAM vs. Reality*, p. 17.

[10] Steven A. Camarota, *Estimating the Impact of the DREAM Act*, Center for Immigration Studies, December 2010, http://www.cis.org.

[11] See description of S. 729 and S. 3827 in "Legislation in the 111th Congress" in **Appendix**.

surpassing a high school grade point average (GPA) threshold. Although admissions applications for most colleges and universities request that students provide their Social Security numbers, this information typically is not required for admission.

Even if they are able to gain admission, however, unauthorized alien students often find it difficult, if not impossible, to pay for higher education. Under the Higher Education Act (HEA) of 1965, as amended, they are ineligible for federal financial aid.[12] In most instances, unauthorized alien students are likewise ineligible for state financial aid. Furthermore, as explained in the next section, they also may be ineligible for in-state tuition.

1996 Provision

Section 505 of IIRIRA places restrictions on state provision of educational benefits to unauthorized aliens. It directs that an unauthorized alien

> shall not be eligible on the basis of residence within a State (or a political subdivision) for any postsecondary education benefit unless a citizen or national of the United States is eligible for such a benefit (in no less an amount, duration, and scope) without regard to whether the citizen or national is such a resident.

There is disagreement about the meaning of this provision, and no authoritative guidance is available in either congressional report language or federal regulations.[13] The conference report on the bill containing IIRIRA did not explain §505. (A conference report on a predecessor IIRIRA bill, which contained a section identical to §505, described the section as "provid[ing] that illegal aliens are not eligible for in-state tuition rates at public institutions of higher education."[14]) Some observers have argued that Congress exceeded its authority in §505 by legislating on how states can dispense state benefits.[15]

Although §505 does not refer explicitly to the granting of "in-state" residency status for tuition purposes and some question whether it even covers in-state tuition, the debate surrounding §505 has focused on the provision of in-state tuition rates to unauthorized aliens. A key issue in this debate is whether it is possible to grant in-state tuition to resident unauthorized students (and not to all citizens) without violating §505. Various states have attempted to do this. For example, a California law passed in 2001 makes unauthorized aliens eligible for in-state tuition at state community colleges and California State University campuses.[16] The measure, however, bases eligibility on criteria that do not explicitly include state residency. The requirements to qualify for

---

[12] The HEA is P.L. 89-329, November 8, 1965, 20 U.S.C. §1001 *et seq.* Section 484(a)(5) sets forth immigration-related eligibility requirements for federal student financial aid, and §484(g) requires the U.S. Department of Education to verify the immigration status of applicants for federal financial aid. Also see U.S. Department of Education, Office of Federal Student Aid, *Federal Student Aid Handbook 2011-2012*, Volume 1 (Student Eligibility), Chapter 2 (Citizenship), http://ifap.ed.gov/fsahandbook/attachments/1112FSAHbkVol1Ch2.pdf.

[13] No implementing regulations on §505 have been issued.

[14] U.S. Congress, House Conference Committee, *Illegal Immigration Reform and Immigrant Responsibility Act of 1996*, conference report to accompany H.R. 2202, 104th Cong., 2nd sess., H.Rept. 104-828, p. 240.

[15] See, for example, Dawn Konet, "Unauthorized Youths and Higher Education: The Ongoing Debate," Migration Information Source, Migration Policy Institute, September 2007, http://www.migrationinformation.org/Feature/display.cfm?ID=642.

[16] Cal. Educ. Code §68130.5. The law does not apply to the University of California system.

---

in-state tuition under the California law include attendance at a California high school for at least three years and either graduation from a California high school "or attainment of the equivalent thereof." In addition, the law requires an unauthorized alien student to file an affidavit stating that he or she either has filed an application to legalize his or her status or will file such an application as soon as he or she is eligible. California officials have argued that by using eligibility criteria other than state residency, the law does not violate the §505 prohibition on conferring educational benefits on the basis of state residency. In November 2010, the California Supreme Court upheld the California law. At least one federal court also has considered whether state laws that authorize in-state tuition for unauthorized students violate §505.[17]

Action in the 112th Congress

Similar, but not identical, Senate and House DREAM Act bills (S. 952, H.R. 1842) have been introduced in the 112th Congress. Although there are differences between the bills, both are entitled the Development, Relief, and Education for Alien Minors (DREAM) Act of 2011. Both likewise take a step back from some of the revisions incorporated in the DREAM Act measure approved by the House in the 111th Congress[18] and, as discussed below, include some more traditional DREAM Act provisions. By contrast, another House bill that would legalize the status of unauthorized alien students (H.R. 3823) more closely resembles the version of the DREAM Act approved by the House in 2010.

S. 952

S. 952, the DREAM Act of 2011, was introduced by Senator Durbin with 32 original cosponsors. It would repeal IIRIRA §505 and thereby eliminate the restriction on state provision of postsecondary educational benefits to unauthorized aliens. It also would enable eligible unauthorized students (including those in temporary protected status under the INA[19]) to adjust to LPR status in the United States through an immigration procedure known as cancellation of removal. Cancellation of removal is a discretionary form of relief that an alien can apply for while in removal proceedings before an immigration judge. If cancellation of removal is granted, the alien's status is adjusted to that of an LPR. S. 952 would enable aliens to affirmatively apply for cancellation of removal without first being placed in removal proceedings, and it would place no limit on the number of aliens who could be granted cancellation of removal/adjustment of status under its provisions.

To be eligible for cancellation of removal/adjustment of status under S. 952, an alien would have to demonstrate that he or she had been continuously physically present in the United States for

---

[17] For additional information, see CRS Report RS22500, *Unauthorized Alien Students, Higher Education, and In-State Tuition Rates A Legal Analysis*.

[18] See description of House-approved DREAM Act Language and H.R. 6497 in "Legislation in the 111th Congress" in **Appendix**.

[19] As set forth in INA §244, TPS is blanket relief that may be granted under the following conditions: there is ongoing armed conflict posing serious threat to personal safety; a foreign state requests TPS because it temporarily cannot handle the return of nationals due to environmental disaster; or there are extraordinary and temporary conditions in a foreign state that prevent aliens from returning, provided that granting TPS is consistent with U.S. national interests. See CRS Report RS20844, *Temporary Protected Status Current Immigration Policy and Issues*, by Ruth Ellen Wasem and Karma Ester.

five years immediately preceding the date of enactment of the act; was age 15 or younger at the time of initial entry; had been a person of good moral character since the time of initial entry; and was age 35 or younger on the date of enactment. The alien also would have to demonstrate that he or she had been admitted to an institution of higher education in the United States or had earned a high school diploma or the equivalent in the United States.

Aliens applying for relief under S. 952 would be subject to special requirements concerning inadmissibility. The INA enumerates classes of inadmissible aliens. Under the INA, except as otherwise provided, aliens who are inadmissible under specified grounds, such as health-related grounds or criminal grounds, are ineligible to receive visas from the Department of State or to be admitted to the United States by the Department of Homeland Security.[20] S. 952 specifies the grounds of inadmissibility that would apply to aliens seeking relief.[21] An alien applying for cancellation of removal/adjustment of status under S. 952 would have to show that he or she was not inadmissible on INA criminal, security, smuggling, student visa abuse, citizenship ineligibility, polygamy, international child abduction, or unlawful voting grounds.[22] Applicants also would need to satisfy requirements concerning convictions for offenses under federal or state law. In addition, they would have to submit biometric and biographic data, which would be used to conduct background checks, and would need to register under the Military Selective Service Act, if applicable.

S. 952 would require that applications for cancellation of removal/adjustment of status be filed not later than one year after the date the alien earned a high school diploma or the equivalent, or the effective date of final regulations, whichever is later. Under the bill, the Secretary of Homeland Security or the Attorney General could not remove an alien with a pending application who establishes prima facie eligibility for relief. In addition, the Attorney General would stay the removal proceedings of an alien who is at least age five,[23] meets all the eligibility requirements except high school graduation, and is enrolled in primary or secondary school.

Aliens granted cancellation of removal under S. 952 would be adjusted initially to *conditional* permanent resident status. Such conditional status would be valid for six years and would be subject to termination. To have the condition removed and become a full-fledged LPR, an alien would have to submit an application during a specified period and meet additional requirements. Among these requirements, the alien would need to have demonstrated good moral character during the period of conditional permanent residence; could not have abandoned his or her U.S. residence; and would need either to have earned a degree from an institution of higher education (or to have completed at least two years in a bachelor's or higher degree program) in the United States or to have served in the uniformed services[24] for at least two years. Other requirements for removal of the condition include satisfaction of the English language and civics requirements for

---

[20] The INA grounds of inadmissibility are in INA §212(a). See CRS Report R41104, *Immigration Visa Issuances and Grounds for Exclusion Policy and Trends*, by Ruth Ellen Wasem.

[21] Unlike DREAM Act bills in prior Congresses, S. 952 does not specify grounds of deportability that would apply to aliens seeking relief. The INA grounds of deportability are in INA §237(a).

[22] The Secretary of Homeland Security would have the authority to waive specified grounds for humanitarian, family unity, or public interest purposes.

[23] This age five cutoff is a departure from past DREAM Act bills, which typically limited protections from removal to potential beneficiaries who were at least age 12.

[24] As defined in Section 101(a) of Title 10 of the U.S. Code, the term *uniformed services* means the Armed Forces (Army, Navy, Air Force, Marine Corps, and Coast Guard); the commissioned corps of the National Oceanic and Atmospheric Administration; and the commissioned corps of the Public Health Service.

naturalization, submission of biometric and biographic data, and completion of background checks.

The time an alien spent as a conditional LPR would count for naturalization purposes under S. 952. Typically, an alien must be in LPR status for five years before he or she can naturalize. Under S. 952, however, the condition on the LPR status would have to be removed before an alien could apply for naturalization.

S. 952 would place restrictions on the eligibility of aliens who have conditional LPR status under the bill for federal student financial aid under Title IV of the Higher Education Act of 1965, as amended. Aliens with conditional LPR status would be eligible only for student loans, federal work-study programs, and services (such as counseling, tutorial services, and mentoring), subject to the applicable requirements. They would be ineligible for federal Pell Grants or federal supplemental educational opportunity grants.

H.R. 1842

H.R. 1842, the DREAM Act of 2011, was introduced by Representative Berman with bipartisan cosponsorship. It is similar in many respects to S. 952, but different in some areas. Like the Senate bill, it would repeal IIRIRA §505 and thereby eliminate the restriction on state provision of postsecondary educational benefits to unauthorized aliens. It also would enable eligible unauthorized students to adjust to LPR status in the United States through cancellation of removal. Unlike S. 952, it would not provide for adjustment to LPR status for aliens in temporary protected status. Like S. 952, it would enable aliens to affirmatively apply for cancellation of removal without first being placed in removal proceedings, and it would place no limit on the number of aliens who could be granted cancellation of removal/adjustment of status.

H.R. 1842 includes many of the same requirements as S. 952 for cancellation of removal/ adjustment of status. Under the House bill, as under the Senate bill, an alien would have to demonstrate that he or she had been physically present continuously in the United States for not less than five years immediately preceding the date of enactment of the act; was age 15 or younger at the time of initial entry; had been a person of good moral character since the time of initial entry; and had been admitted to an institution of higher education in the United States or had earned a high school diploma or the equivalent in the United States. Under H.R. 1842, the alien would need to demonstrate that he or she was age 32 or younger on the date of enactment, compared to age 35 or younger under the Senate bill.

With respect to the INA grounds of inadmissibility, an alien applying for relief under H.R. 1842, as under S. 952, would have to show that he or she was not inadmissible on INA criminal, security, smuggling, student visa abuse, citizenship ineligibility, polygamy, international child abduction, or unlawful voting grounds.[25] An additional ground of inadmissibility—the public charge ground—would apply under the House bill. As under S. 952, applicants for relief under H.R. 1842 would have to submit biometric and biographic data, which would be used to conduct background checks, and would need to register under the Military Selective Service Act, if applicable. They would not be subject to requirements like those in S. 952 concerning convictions for offenses under federal or state law.

---

[25] The Secretary of Homeland Security would have the authority to waive the criminal grounds for humanitarian, family unity, or public interest purposes.

The provisions in H.R. 1842 concerning the application process and protection from removal for potential beneficiaries are very similar to those in S. 952. Like S. 952, the House bill would require that applications be filed not later than one year after the date the alien earned a high school diploma or the equivalent, or the effective date of final regulations, whichever is later. Under the House bill, the Secretary of Homeland Security or the Attorney General could not remove an alien with a pending application who establishes prima facie eligibility for relief. In addition, the Attorney General would stay the removal proceedings of an alien who is at least age 12 (compared to the age five cutoff in S. 952), meets all the eligibility requirements except high school graduation, and is enrolled in primary or secondary school.

Aliens granted cancellation of removal under H.R. 1842, as under S. 952, would be adjusted initially to *conditional* permanent resident status. Such conditional status would be valid for six years and would be subject to termination. To have the condition removed and become a full-fledged LPR, an alien would have to submit an application during a specified period and meet additional requirements. Among these requirements, the alien would need to have demonstrated good moral character during the period of conditional permanent residence; could not have abandoned his or her U.S. residence; and would need either to have earned a degree from an institution of higher education (or to have completed at least two years in a bachelor's or higher degree program) in the United States or to have served in the uniformed services for at least two years. Other requirements for removal of the condition include satisfaction of the English language and civics requirements for naturalization, submission of biometric and biographic data, and completion of background checks. The time an alien spent as a conditional LPR would count for naturalization purposes under H.R. 1842, but the condition on the LPR status would have to be removed before an alien could apply for naturalization.

H.R. 1842 would place temporary restrictions on the eligibility of aliens who adjust to LPR status under its provisions for federal student financial aid under Title IV of the Higher Education Act of 1965, as amended. Aliens adjusting status under the bill who are in conditional permanent resident status would be eligible for student loans, federal work-study programs, and services, but they would not be eligible for federal Pell Grants and federal supplemental educational opportunity grants.

H.R. 3823

H.R. 3823, the Adjusted Residency for Military Service (ARMS) Act, was introduced by Representative Rivera. As mentioned above, it is similar in many respects to the DREAM Act language approved by the House as part of H.R. 5281 in the 111th Congress,[26] and it is significantly different than S. 952 and H.R. 1842.

H.R. 3823 has less of an educational component than S. 952 and H.R. 1842, or even the House-passed measure in the 111th Congress. Unlike S. 952 and H.R. 1842, H.R. 3823 would not repeal IIRIRA §505 and thus would not eliminate the statutory restriction on state provision of postsecondary educational benefits to unauthorized aliens. Unlike S. 952, H.R. 1842, and the House-approved measure in the 111th Congress, as detailed below, H.R. 3823 would require unauthorized alien students to perform military service in order to obtain LPR status. They could not pursue higher education instead.

---

[26] See description of House-approved DREAM Act Language and H.R. 6497 in "Legislation in the 111th Congress" in **Appendix**.

Under H.R. 3823, as under the House-approved DREAM Act language in the 111th Congress, an eligible alien could go though the cancellation of removal procedure and be granted conditional *nonimmigrant* status. Unlike under S. 952, H.R. 1842, and most other DREAM Act bills introduced in past Congresses, the alien's status would not be adjusted to that of a conditional LPR.

Like most other DREAM Act bills, H.R. 3823 would enable an alien to affirmatively apply for cancellation of removal without first being placed in removal proceedings, would establish a deadline for submitting initial cancellation of removal applications, and would prohibit the Secretary of Homeland Security from removing an alien with a pending application who establishes prima facie eligibility for relief. Unlike other DREAM Act bills, H.R. 3823 does not include provisions about staying the removal proceedings of alien children who are enrolled in primary or secondary school and who meet all the eligibility requirements for initial conditional status except high school graduation.

To be eligible for cancellation of removal/conditional nonimmigrant status under H.R. 3823, an alien would need to demonstrate that he or she had been physically present in the United States for a continuous period of not less than five years immediately preceding the date of enactment of the legislation, had not yet reached age 16 at the time of initial entry, had been a person of good moral character since the date of initial entry, and was younger than age 30 on the date of enactment. These requirements are the same as in S. 952 and H.R. 1842 except for the maximum age limitation on the date of enactment.[27] Under H.R. 3823, the alien would also have to demonstrate that he or she had been admitted to an institution of higher education in the United States, or had earned a high school diploma or the equivalent in the United States, as under both S. 952 and H.R. 1842, and that he or she had never been under a final administrative or judicial order of exclusion, deportation, or removal, with some exceptions.

H.R. 3823 specifies the grounds of inadmissibility and deportability that would apply to aliens seeking relief. An alien applying for cancellation of removal/conditional nonimmigrant status under the bill would have to show that he or she was not inadmissible on INA health-related, criminal, security, public charge, smuggling, student visa abuse, citizenship ineligibility, polygamy, international child abduction, or unlawful voting grounds, and was not deportable on INA criminal, security, smuggling, marriage fraud, public charge, or unlawful voting grounds.[28] Applicants would also need to satisfy requirements concerning convictions for offenses under federal or state law. In addition, they would have to submit biometric and biographic data, which would be used to conduct background checks, and would need to register under the Military Selective Service Act, if applicable.

As noted above, an alien whose removal is cancelled under H.R. 3823 would be granted conditional nonimmigrant status, as opposed to conditional LPR status under S. 952 and H.R. 1842. Such conditional nonimmigrant status would be valid for an initial period of five years and would be subject to termination. Among the grounds for termination would be failure to

---

[27] Under H.R. 1842, an alien would have to be age 32 or younger; under S. 952, an alien would have to be age 35 or younger.

[28] The Secretary of Homeland Security would have the authority to waive some of these grounds of inadmissibility and deportability for humanitarian, family unity, or public interest purposes.

successfully enlist in the Armed Forces[29] within nine months after being granted conditional status.

Under H.R. 3823, an alien's conditional nonimmigrant status would be extended for a second five-year period (for a total conditional period of 10 years) if the alien meets the following requirements: demonstration of good moral character as a conditional nonimmigrant; compliance with the bill's inadmissibility and deportability provisions discussed above; no abandonment of U.S. residence; and service in the Armed Forces on active duty for at least two years or service in a reserve component of the Armed Forces in active status for at least four years.

By comparison, under the House-approved measure in the 111th Congress there would also be two five-year conditional nonimmigrant status periods and beneficiaries would have to meet a set of requirements to have their status extended for the second five-year period. With respect to the requirements for extension, however, the House-approved measure included different military service requirements than H.R. 3823 and, unlike that bill, would give beneficiaries the option of completing two years of higher education instead of serving in the Armed Forces.

Another similarity to the DREAM Act language approved in the 111th Congress, and a difference from S. 952, H.R. 1842, and other DREAM Act bills, is that H.R. 3823 would establish surcharges on applications for relief. There would be a surcharge of $525 on each application for cancellation of removal/conditional nonimmigrant status, and a surcharge of $2,000 on each application for an extension of conditional nonimmigrant status.

At the end of the second period of conditional nonimmigrant status, as specified, the alien could apply for adjustment to LPR status. Among the requirements for adjustment of status, the alien would need to have demonstrated good moral character during the period of conditional nonimmigrant status, be in compliance with the bill's inadmissibility and deportability provisions, and could not have abandoned his or her U.S. residence. In addition, applicants for adjustment of status under H.R. 3823, as under the House-approved version of the DREAM Act in the 111th Congress, would need to satisfy the English language and civic requirements for naturalization, satisfy any applicable federal tax liability, submit biometric and biographic data, and complete background checks. There would be no limitation on the number of individuals eligible for adjustment of status.

Under H.R. 3823, aliens who adjust status and meet other requirements would be eligible for naturalization after three years in LPR status. Unlike under S. 952 and H.R. 1842, the time spent in conditional status under H.R. 3823 (during which the aliens would be conditional nonimmigrants) would not count for naturalization purposes.

H.R. 3823 also contains provisions on the treatment for other purposes of aliens who are granted conditional nonimmigrant status or LPR status under the bill. Like the version of the DREAM Act approved by the 111th Congress, H.R. 3823 provides that conditional nonimmigrants are to be considered lawfully present for all purposes except for provisions in the Patient Protection and Affordable Care Act (PPACA), as enacted by the 111th Congress,[30] concerning premium tax

---

[29] The term *Armed Forces*, as defined in Section 101(a) of Title 10 of the U.S. Code, means the Army, Navy, Air Force, Marine Corps, and Coast Guard.

[30] P.L. 111-148, March 23, 2010.

credits and cost sharing subsidies.[31] It also provides that aliens who adjust to LPR status under the bill would be deemed to have completed the five-year period required for LPR eligibility for certain types of federal public assistance, as established by the Personal Responsibility and Work Opportunity Reconciliation Act (PWORA) of 1996.[32] Unlike DREAM Act bills that provide a higher education route to LPR status, H.R. 3823 contains no provisions on eligibility of aliens who adjust status under its provisions for federal student financial aid.

Pro/Con Arguments

Those who favor DREAM Act proposals to repeal §505 and grant LPR status to unauthorized alien students offer a variety of arguments. They maintain that it is both fair and in the U.S. national interest to enable unauthorized alien students who graduate from high school to continue their education. And they emphasize that large numbers will be unable to do so unless they are eligible for in-state tuition rates at colleges in their states of residence.

Advocates for unauthorized alien students argue that many of them were brought into the United States at a very young age and should not be held responsible for the decision to enter the country illegally. According to these advocates, many of the students have spent most of their lives in the United States and have few, if any, ties to their countries of origin. They argue that these special circumstances demand that the students be granted humanitarian relief in the form of LPR status.

Those who oppose making unauthorized alien students eligible for in-state tuition or legal status emphasize that the students and their families are in the United States illegally and should be removed from the country. They object to using U.S. taxpayer money to subsidize the education of individuals (through the granting of in-state tuition rates) who are in the United States in violation of the law. They maintain that funding the education of these students should be the responsibility of their parents or their home countries. They further argue that it is unfair to charge unauthorized alien students in-state tuition while charging some U.S. citizens higher out-of-state rates.

More broadly, these opponents argue that granting benefits to unauthorized alien students rewards lawbreakers and thereby undermines the U.S. immigration system. In their view, the availability of benefits, especially LPR status, will encourage more illegal immigration into the country.[33]

---

[31] For information on the PPACA provisions, see CRS Report R41714, *Treatment of Noncitizens Under the Patient Protection and Affordable Care Act*, by Alison Siskin.

[32] For information on current eligibility policy, see CRS Report RL33809, *Noncitizen Eligibility for Federal Public Assistance Policy Overview and Trends*, by Ruth Ellen Wasem.

[33] For pro and con arguments, see, for example, Jerry Gonzalez and Phil Kent, "Should Congress Pass DREAM Act for Immigrant Children?," *Atlanta Journal-Constitution*, November 23, 2010; Stacy Teicher Khadaroo, "Why DREAM Act Passed House, But May Fall in Senate," *Christian Science Monitor*, December 9, 2010; and Brad Knickerbocker, "DREAM Act Poised for Senate Vote Saturday," *Christian Science Monitor*, December 17, 2010.

Appendix. Action in the 109th, 110th, and 111th Congresses

Many DREAM Act bills seeking to provide relief to unauthorized alien students by repealing the 1996 provision and enabling certain unauthorized alien students to obtain LPR status have been introduced in recent Congresses. In both the 107th and 108th Congresses, the Senate Judiciary Committee reported DREAM Act legislation.[34]

Legislation in the 109th Congress

In the 109th Congress, Senator Durbin introduced the Development, Relief, and Education for Alien Minors (DREAM) Act of 2005 (S. 2075), and Representative Lincoln Diaz-Balart introduced the American Dream Act (H.R. 5131). Both bills had bipartisan cosponsorship.

Both S. 2075 and H.R. 5131 would have repealed IIRIRA §505 and thereby eliminated the restriction on state provision of postsecondary educational benefits to unauthorized aliens. Both bills also would have enabled eligible unauthorized students to adjust to LPR status in the United States through the cancellation of removal procedure. S. 2075 and H.R. 5131 would have allowed aliens to affirmatively apply for cancellation of removal without being placed in removal proceedings. There would have been no limit on the number of aliens who could be granted cancellation of removal/adjustment of status under the bills.

Among the eligibility requirements for cancellation of removal/adjustment of status in both S. 2075 and H.R. 5131, the alien would have had to demonstrate that he or she had been physically present in the United States for a continuous period of not less than five years immediately preceding the date of enactment, had not yet reached age 16 at the time of initial entry, and had been a person of good moral character since the time of application. The alien also would have been required to demonstrate that he or she had been admitted to an institution of higher education in the United States, or had earned a high school diploma or the equivalent in the United States.

The eligibility requirements for cancellation of removal/adjustment of status in S. 2075 and H.R. 5131 differed with respect to the applicable INA grounds of inadmissibility and deportability.[35] S. 2075 and H.R. 5131 each specified which of the inadmissibility and deportability grounds would have applied to aliens seeking to adjust status under its provisions. A greater number of these grounds would have applied under S. 2075 than H.R. 5131. In addition, to be eligible under S. 2075, an alien could never have been under a final administrative or judicial order of exclusion, deportation, or removal, with some exceptions.

An alien granted cancellation of removal under S. 2075 and H.R. 5131 would have been adjusted initially to conditional permanent resident status. Such conditional status would have been valid for six years and would have been subject to termination. To have the condition removed and become a full-fledged LPR, the alien would have had to submit an application during a specified

---

[34] For further information and analysis, see archived CRS Report RL31365, *Unauthorized Alien Students Legislation in the 107th and 108th Congresses*, by Andorra Bruno and Jeffrey J. Kuenzi.

[35] The INA grounds of inadmissibility are in INA §212(a), and the INA grounds of deportability are in INA §237(a).

period and meet additional requirements. These requirements would have included that the alien had demonstrated good moral character during the period of conditional permanent residence; had not abandoned his or her U.S. residence; and had either acquired a college degree (or completed at least two years in a bachelor's or higher degree program) in the United States, or had served in the uniformed services for at least two years.

Both S. 2075 and H.R. 5131 would have placed restrictions on aliens who adjusted to LPR status under their provisions, with respect to eligibility for federal student financial aid under Title IV of the Higher Education Act of 1965, as amended. S. 2075 would have made aliens who adjusted to LPR status under the bill eligible only for student loans, federal work-study programs, and services (such as counseling, tutorial services, and mentoring), subject to the applicable requirements. Thus, they would not have been eligible for federal Pell Grants or federal supplemental educational opportunity grants. H.R. 5131 would have imposed similar restrictions on eligibility for federal student financial aid, but they would have been temporary. This bill would have made aliens adjusting status under its terms ineligible for federal Pell Grants and federal supplemental educational opportunity grants while they were in conditional permanent resident status. Once the conditional basis of their LPR status was removed, these restrictions would no longer have applied.

The 109th Congress took no action on S. 2075 or H.R. 5131. S. 2075, however, was incorporated into the Comprehensive Immigration Reform Act of 2006 (S. 2611) as Title VI, Subtitle C. S. 2611 passed the Senate on May 25, 2006, but saw no further action. The major immigration bill passed by the House in the 109th Congress, the Border Protection, Antiterrorism, and Illegal Immigration Control Act (H.R. 4437), did not contain any provisions on unauthorized alien students.

Legislation in the 110th Congress

DREAM Act legislation was introduced in the 110th Congress, both in stand-alone bills and as part of larger comprehensive immigration reform measures. A selected number of these bills are described here. Neither the House or Senate passed any of these bills. As discussed below, the Senate failed to invoke cloture on two measures: S. 1639, a bipartisan comprehensive immigration reform proposal that included a DREAM Act title, and S. 2205, a stand-alone DREAM Act bill.

S. 774 and H.R. 1275

The DREAM Act of 2007 (S. 774), introduced by Senator Durbin, and the American Dream Act (H.R. 1275), introduced by Representative Berman, were similar, but not identical, measures. Both had bipartisan cosponsors. Both also were highly similar, respectively, to S. 2075 and H.R. 5131 in the 109th Congress.

S. 774 and H.R. 1275 would have repealed IIRIRA §505 and thereby eliminated the restriction on state provision of postsecondary educational benefits to unauthorized aliens. Both bills also would have enabled eligible unauthorized students to adjust to LPR status in the United States through cancellation of removal. Under S. 774 and H.R. 1275, aliens could have affirmatively applied for cancellation of removal without being placed in removal proceedings. There would have been no limit on the number of aliens who could be granted cancellation of removal/ adjustment of status under the bills.

To be eligible for cancellation of removal/adjustment of status under S. 774 or H.R. 1275, an alien would have had to satisfy a set of requirements. Under both bills, the alien would have had to demonstrate that he or she had been physically present in the United States for a continuous period of not less than five years immediately preceding the date of enactment, had not yet reached age 16 at the time of initial entry, and had been a person of good moral character since the time of application. Both bills also would have required the alien to demonstrate that he or she had been admitted to an institution of higher education in the United States, or had earned a high school diploma or the equivalent in the United States.

Other requirements for cancellation of removal/adjustment of status under S. 774 and H.R. 1275 concerned the INA grounds of inadmissibility and deportability. The eligibility requirements with respect to deportability from the United States were the same in both bills, while the requirements with respect to inadmissibility to the country differed somewhat. To be eligible for cancellation of removal/adjustment of status under either S. 774 or H.R. 1275, an alien would have had to demonstrate that he or she was not inadmissible or deportable on INA criminal, security, or smuggling grounds. S. 774 would have further required that the alien not be inadmissible on international child abduction grounds. In addition, to be eligible for cancellation of removal/adjustment of status under S. 774, an alien could never have been under a final administrative or judicial order of exclusion, deportation, or removal, with some exceptions.

Aliens granted cancellation of removal under S. 774 or H.R. 1275 would have been adjusted initially to conditional permanent resident status. Such conditional status would have been valid for six years and would have been subject to termination. To have the condition removed and become a full-fledged LPR, an alien would have had to submit an application during a specified period and meet additional requirements. Among these requirements, the alien would have needed to demonstrate good moral character during the period of conditional permanent residence; could not have abandoned his or her U.S. residence; and would have needed either a college degree (or to have completed at least two years in a bachelor's or higher degree program) in the United States, or to have served in the uniformed services for at least two years.

Both S. 774 and H.R. 1275 would have placed restrictions on the eligibility of aliens who adjusted to LPR status under their provisions, for federal student financial aid under Title IV of the Higher Education Act of 1965, as amended. S. 774 would have made aliens who adjusted to LPR status under the bill eligible only for student loans, federal work-study programs, and services (such as counseling, tutorial services, and mentoring), subject to the applicable requirements. Thus, they would not have been eligible for federal Pell Grants or federal supplemental educational opportunity grants. H.R. 1275 would have imposed similar restrictions on eligibility for federal student financial aid, but they would have been temporary. Aliens adjusting status under the House bill would have been ineligible for federal Pell Grants and federal supplemental educational opportunity grants while in conditional permanent resident status. Once the conditional basis was removed and they became full-fledged LPRs, these restrictions would no longer have applied.

H.R. 1645

The Security Through Regularized Immigration and a Vibrant Economy Act of 2007, or the STRIVE Act of 2007 (H.R. 1645), introduced by Representative Gutierrez for himself and a bipartisan group of cosponsors, contained DREAM Act provisions in Title VI, Subtitle B. These provisions were nearly identical to S. 774, as discussed above.

H.R. 1221

The Education Access for Rightful Noncitizens (EARN) Act (H.R. 1221), introduced by Representative Gillmor, was a version of the DREAM Act. It was similar in some ways to the bills described above and significantly different in other respects. Like S. 774, H.R. 1275, and H.R. 1645, it would have enabled eligible unauthorized students to adjust to LPR status in the United States through cancellation of removal. Under H.R. 1221, as under these other bills, aliens could have affirmatively applied for cancellation of removal without being placed in removal proceedings, and there would have been no limit on the number of aliens who could be granted cancellation of removal/adjustment of status as specified.

Many of the eligibility requirements for cancellation of removal/adjustment of status—including the physical presence, age at entry, good moral character, and educational requirements—were the same under H.R. 1221, S. 774, H.R. 1275, and H.R. 1645. There were differences, however, with respect to the INA grounds of inadmissibility and deportability. Under H.R. 1221, as under these other bills, aliens would have been ineligible for cancellation of removal/adjustment of status if they were inadmissible or deportable on criminal, security, or smuggling grounds. They also would have been ineligible under H.R. 1221 if they were inadmissible on other grounds, including failure to attend a removal proceeding, or deportable on other grounds, including marriage fraud. In addition, aliens would have been ineligible for cancellation of removal/adjustment of status under H.R. 1221, as under S. 774 and H.R. 1645, if they had ever been under a final administrative or judicial order of exclusion, deportation, or removal, with some exceptions.

As under S. 774, H.R. 1275, and H.R. 1645, aliens granted cancellation of removal under H.R. 1221 would have been adjusted initially to a conditional permanent resident status, which would have been valid for six years. To have the condition removed and become a full-fledged LPR, an alien would have had to submit an application during a specified period and meet additional requirements regarding good moral character, no abandonment of U.S. residence, and higher education or service in the uniformed services, among others, as described above in the "S. 774 and H.R. 1275" section.

At the same time, H.R. 1221 did not contain certain key provisions included in S. 774, H.R. 1275, and H.R. 1645. Unlike these other bills, it would not have placed restrictions on the eligibility of aliens who adjusted to LPR status under its terms, for federal student financial aid. Also unlike S. 774, H.R. 1275, and H.R. 1645, it would not have repealed IIRIRA §505 and thus would not have eliminated the restriction on state provision of postsecondary educational benefits to unauthorized aliens.

S. 1639

A version of the DREAM Act was included in a bipartisan comprehensive immigration reform bill (S. 1639) introduced by Senator Kennedy for himself and Senator Specter. The DREAM Act provisions comprised Title VI, Subtitle B, of S. 1639. The Senate failed to invoke cloture on the measure in June 2007, and the bill was pulled from the Senate floor.

The S. 1639 version of the DREAM Act was substantially different than the other DREAM Act bills in the 110th Congress. The DREAM Act provisions in S. 1639 were tied to other provisions in Title VI of the bill that would have enabled certain unauthorized aliens in the United States to obtain legal status under a new "Z" nonimmigrant visa category. Among the eligibility requirements for Z status, an alien would have had to be continuously physically present in the United States since January 1, 2007, and could not have been lawfully present on that date under any nonimmigrant classification or any other immigration status made available under a treaty or other multinational agreement ratified by the Senate.[36]

S. 1639's DREAM Act title would have established a special adjustment of status mechanism for aliens who were determined to be eligible for, or who had been issued, probationary Z[37] or Z visas, and who met other requirements, including being under age 30 on the date of enactment, being under age 16 at the time of initial entry into the United States, and having either acquired a college degree (or completed at least two years in a bachelor's or higher degree program) in the United States or served in the uniformed services for at least two years. The Secretary of the Department of Homeland Security could have begun adjusting the status of eligible individuals to LPR status three years after the date of enactment.[38] Unlike under the other DREAM Act bills discussed above, DREAM Act beneficiaries under S. 1639 would not have adjusted status through the cancellation of removal procedure and would not have been adjusted initially to conditional permanent resident status.

In other respects, the DREAM Act adjustment of status provisions in S. 1639 were similar to those in the other DREAM Act bills before the 110th Congress. As under the other bills, there would have been no limit on the number of aliens who could have adjusted to LPR status under S. 1639. With respect to federal student financial aid, beneficiaries of the S. 1639 provisions, like beneficiaries under S. 774 and H.R. 1645, would have been eligible for student loans, federal work-study programs, and services (such as counseling, tutorial services, and mentoring), subject to the applicable requirements, but would not have been eligible for grants.[39]

S. 1639, like most other DREAM Act bills before the 110th Congress, coupled adjustment of status provisions for unauthorized students with provisions addressing IIRIRA §505, which, as explained above, places restrictions on state provision of educational benefits to unauthorized aliens. Unlike S. 774, H.R. 1275, and H.R. 1645, however, S. 1639 would not have completely repealed IIRIRA §505. Instead, §616(a) of S. 1639 proposed to make §505 inapplicable with respect to aliens with probationary Z or Z status.

S. 2205

Another version of the DREAM Act (S. 2205) was introduced in October 2007 by Senator Durbin. It contained legalization provisions similar to those in S. 774, H.R. 1275, H.R. 1645, and

---

[36] For further information about the proposed Z classifications, see CRS Report RL32044, *Immigration Policy Considerations Related to Guest Worker Programs*, by Andorra Bruno.

[37] Under S. 1639 §601, certain applicants for Z status would have been eligible to receive probationary benefits in the form of employment authorization pending final adjudication of their applications.

[38] Unlike Z aliens applying to adjust to LPR status under S. 1639 §602, beneficiaries of the DREAM Act provisions would not have been subject to a "back of the line" provision requiring them to wait to adjust status until immigrant visas became available to others whose petitions had been filed by a specified date. Under S. 1639 §602(a)(5), a Z alien could not adjust status to that of an LPR under §602 until 30 days after an immigrant visa became available for approved family-based or employment-based petitions filed before May 1, 2005. For further information about the permanent immigration system, see CRS Report RL32235, *U.S. Immigration Policy on Permanent Admissions*, by Ruth Ellen Wasem.

[39] Aliens in probationary Z or Z nonimmigrant status who met certain requirements similarly would have been eligible for student loans, federal work-study programs, and services, but not grants.

H.R. 1221. Under S. 2205, eligible unauthorized students could have adjusted to LPR status through cancellation of removal. Aliens could have applied affirmatively for cancellation of removal without being placed in removal proceedings, and there would have been no limit on the number of aliens who could be granted cancellation of removal/adjustment of status, as specified.

To be eligible for cancellation of removal/adjustment of status under S. 2205, an alien would have had to demonstrate, among other requirements, that he or she had been physically present in the United States for a continuous period of not less than five years immediately preceding the date of enactment, had not yet reached age 16 at the time of initial entry, had been a person of good moral character since the date of enactment, and had been admitted to an institution of higher education in the United States or had earned a high school diploma or the equivalent in the United States. In addition, in a requirement not in S. 774, H.R. 1275, H.R. 1221, or H.R. 1645 but included in S. 1639, the alien would also have had to show that he or she was under age 30 on the date of enactment. The eligibility requirements in S. 2205 with respect to the INA grounds of inadmissibility and deportability were similar to those in H.R. 1221, as discussed above. Also like H.R. 1221 and most of the other DREAM Act bills before the 110th Congress, S. 2205 would have made ineligible, aliens who had ever been under a final administrative or judicial order of exclusion, deportation, or removal, with some exceptions.

An alien granted cancellation of removal under S. 2205 would have been adjusted initially to conditional permanent resident status. To have the condition removed and become a full-fledged LPR, the alien would have had to meet additional requirements, including acquisition of a college degree (or completion of at least two years in a bachelor's or higher degree program) or service in the uniformed services for at least two years.

A key difference between S. 2205 on the one hand and S. 774, H.R. 1275, and H.R. 1645 on the other was that S. 2205, like H.R. 1221, would not have repealed IIRIRA §505 and thus would not have eliminated the restriction on state provision of postsecondary educational benefits to unauthorized aliens. On October 24, 2007, the Senate voted on a motion to invoke cloture on S. 2205. The motion failed on a vote of 52 to 44.

Legislation in the 111th Congress

Senator Durbin and Representative Berman introduced DREAM Act bills in the 111th Congress. Senator Durbin introduced the Development, Relief, and Education for Alien Minors (DREAM) Act of 2009 (S. 729) and four versions of the Development, Relief, and Education for Alien Minors (DREAM) Act of 2010 (S. 3827, S. 3962, S. 3963, S. 3992). Representative Berman introduced the American Dream Act (H.R. 1751) and the Development, Relief, and Education for Alien Minors (DREAM) Act of 2010 (H.R. 6497). Representative Djou introduced a related bill, the Citizenship and Service Act of 2010 (H.R. 6327).

On December 8, 2010, the House approved DREAM Act language as part of an unrelated bill, the Removal Clarification Act of 2010 (H.R. 5281). On December 18, 2010, the Senate failed to invoke cloture on a motion to agree to the House-passed DREAM Act amendment. The vote on the cloture motion was 55 to 41.[40]

[40] In addition, on December 9, 2010, following House action on H.R. 5281, there was another DREAM Act-related vote in the Senate. That day, the Senate voted, 59-40, to table a motion to proceed to a Senate DREAM Act bill, S. 3992. DREAM Act supporters voted for the tabling motion in an effort to clear the way for the Senate to consider the (continued...)

House-Approved DREAM Act Language and H.R. 6497

The DREAM Act language approved by the House as part of H.R. 5281 was the same as the text of the DREAM Act of 2010 (H.R. 6497), as introduced by Representative Berman, and was similar to the DREAM Act of 2010 (S. 3992), as introduced by Senator Durbin. Like other DREAM Act bills in the 111th Congress, the House-approved DREAM Act amendment to H.R. 5281 would have enabled eligible unauthorized students to adjust to LPR status in the United States, although it would have established a different pathway than most of the other bills. Unlike some other DREAM Act bills introduced in the 111th Congress, the House-approved DREAM Act language would not have repealed IIRIRA §505 and thus would not have eliminated the statutory restriction on state provision of postsecondary educational benefits to unauthorized aliens.

Under the House-approved DREAM Act amendment to H.R. 5281, an eligible alien could have gone though the cancellation of removal procedure and been granted conditional *nonimmigrant* status. Unlike under most other DREAM Act bills in the 111th Congress, as discussed below, the alien's status would not have been adjusted to that of a conditional LPR. The House-approved version of the DREAM Act would have enabled an alien to affirmatively apply for cancellation of removal without first being placed in removal proceedings and also would have established a deadline for submitting initial cancellation of removal applications.

To be eligible for cancellation of removal/conditional nonimmigrant status under the House-approved DREAM Act amendment to H.R. 5281, an alien would have needed to demonstrate that he or she had been physically present in the United States for a continuous period of not less than five years immediately preceding the date of enactment of the legislation, had not yet reached age 16 at the time of initial entry, had been a person of good moral character since the date of initial entry, and was younger than age 30 on the date of enactment. The alien also would have had to demonstrate that he or she had been admitted to an institution of higher education in the United States, or had earned a high school diploma or the equivalent in the United States, and that he or she had never been under a final administrative or judicial order of exclusion, deportation, or removal, with some exceptions.

The House-approved version of the DREAM Act specified the grounds of inadmissibility and deportability that would have applied to aliens seeking relief. An alien applying for cancellation of removal/conditional nonimmigrant status under the House-passed measure would have had to show that he or she was not inadmissible on INA health-related, criminal, security, public charge, smuggling, student visa abuse, citizenship ineligibility, polygamy, international child abduction, or unlawful voting grounds, and was not deportable on INA criminal, security, smuggling, marriage fraud, public charge, or unlawful voting grounds.[41] Applicants also would have needed to satisfy requirements concerning convictions for offenses under federal or state law. In addition, they would have had to submit biometric and biographic data, which would have been used to conduct background checks, and would have needed to register under the Military Selective Service Act, if applicable.

(...continued)

House-approved DREAM Act amendment to H.R. 5281.

[41] The Secretary of Homeland Security would have had the authority to waive some of these grounds of inadmissibility and deportability for humanitarian, family unity, or public interest purposes.

Aliens whose removal was cancelled under the House-approved DREAM Act amendment to H.R. 5281 would have been granted conditional nonimmigrant status. Such conditional status would have been valid for an initial period of five years and would have been subject to termination. An alien's conditional nonimmigrant status would have been extended for a second five-year period if the alien met the following requirements: demonstration of good moral character as a conditional nonimmigrant; compliance with the bill's inadmissibility and deportability provisions discussed above; no abandonment of U.S. residence; and either acquisition of a degree from an institution of higher education (or completion of at least two years in a bachelor's or higher degree program) in the United States, or service in the Armed Forces for at least two years.

Unlike other DREAM Act bills in the 111th Congress, the House-approved DREAM Act amendment to H.R. 5281 would have established surcharges on applications for relief. There would have been a surcharge of $525 on each application for cancellation of removal/conditional nonimmigrant status, and a surcharge of $2,000 on each application for an extension of conditional nonimmigrant status.

At the end of the second period of conditional nonimmigrant status, as specified, the alien could have applied for adjustment to LPR status. Among the requirements for adjustment of status, the alien would have needed to have demonstrated good moral character during the period of conditional nonimmigrant status; would have had to be in compliance with the bill's inadmissibility and deportability provisions; and could not have abandoned his or her U.S. residence. In addition, applicants for adjustment of status under the House-approved version of the DREAM Act would have needed to satisfy the English language and civic requirements for naturalization, satisfy any applicable federal tax liability, submit biometric and biographic data, and complete background checks. There would have been no limitation on the number of individuals eligible for adjustment of status.

Aliens who adjusted status and met other requirements would have been eligible for naturalization after three years in LPR status. Unlike under DREAM Act bills in the 111th Congress that would have granted conditional LPR status, the time spent in conditional status under the House-approved DREAM Act language (during which the aliens would have been conditional nonimmigrants) would not have counted for naturalization purposes.

Like other DREAM Act bills in the 111th Congress, the House-approved DREAM Act amendment to H.R. 5281 would have placed restrictions on the eligibility of aliens who adjusted status under its provisions for federal student financial aid under Title IV of the Higher Education Act of 1965, as amended. Aliens granted conditional nonimmigrant status or LPR status would have been eligible for student loans, federal work-study programs, and services (such as counseling, tutorial services, and mentoring), subject to the applicable requirements. Unlike other LPRs, they would not have been eligible for federal Pell Grants or federal supplemental educational opportunity grants.

The House-approved version of the DREAM Act also contained provisions on the treatment for other purposes of aliens who were granted conditional nonimmigrant status or LPR status under the bill. It provided that conditional nonimmigrants would have been considered lawfully present for all purposes except for provisions in the Patient Protection and Affordable Care Act (PPACA), as enacted by the 111th Congress,[42] concerning premium tax credits and cost sharing subsidies.[43] It

---

[42] P.L. 111-148, March 23, 2010.

also provided that aliens who adjusted to LPR status under the bill would have been deemed to have completed the five-year period required for LPR eligibility for certain types of federal public assistance, as established by the Personal Responsibility and Work Opportunity Reconciliation Act (PWORA) of 1996.[44]

H.R. 1751

The American Dream Act (H.R. 1751), as introduced by Representative Berman, would have repealed IIRIRA §505 and thereby eliminated the restriction on state provision of postsecondary educational benefits to unauthorized aliens. It likewise would have enabled eligible unauthorized students to adjust to LPR status in the United States through the cancellation of removal procedure. Under H.R. 1751, aliens could have applied for cancellation of removal without first being placed in removal proceedings, and there would have been no limit on the number of aliens who could be granted cancellation of removal/adjustment of status.

To be eligible for cancellation of removal/adjustment of status under H.R. 1751, an alien would have had to demonstrate that he or she had been physically present in the United States for a continuous period of not less than five years immediately preceding the date of enactment; had not yet reached age 16 at the time of initial entry; had been a person of good moral character since the time of application; and was not inadmissible or deportable on INA criminal, security, or smuggling grounds. The bill also would have required the alien to demonstrate that he or she had been admitted to an institution of higher education in the United States, or had earned a high school diploma or the equivalent in the United States. Unlike under most other DREAM Act bills in the 111th Congress, however, H.R. 1751 would not have required the alien to show that he or she was under a particular age on the date of enactment. H.R. 1751 also provided for expedited processing of applications without an additional fee.

Aliens granted cancellation of removal under H.R. 1751 would have been adjusted initially to conditional permanent resident status. Such conditional status would have been valid for six years and would have been subject to termination. The time an alien spent as a conditional LPR would have counted for naturalization purposes. (Typically, an alien must be in LPR status for five years before he or she can naturalize.) Under H.R. 1751, however, the condition on the LPR status would have needed to be removed before the alien could apply for naturalization.

To have the condition removed and become a full-fledged LPR, an alien would have had to apply during a specified period and meet additional requirements. Among these requirements, the alien would have had to demonstrate good moral character during the period of conditional permanent residence; could not have abandoned his or her U.S. residence; and would have needed either to have earned a degree from an institution of higher education (or to have completed at least two years in a bachelor's or higher degree program) in the United States, or to have served in the uniformed services for at least two years.

(...continued)

[43] For information on the PPACA provisions, see CRS Report R41714, *Treatment of Noncitizens Under the Patient Protection and Affordable Care Act.*

[44] For information on current eligibility policy, see CRS Report RL33809, *Noncitizen Eligibility for Federal Public Assistance Policy Overview and Trends.*

H.R. 1751 would have placed temporary restrictions on the eligibility of aliens who adjusted to LPR status under its provisions for federal student financial aid under Title IV of the Higher Education Act of 1965, as amended. Aliens adjusting status under the bill would have been eligible for student loans, federal work-study programs, and services, but they would not have been eligible for federal Pell Grants and federal supplemental educational opportunity grants while in conditional permanent resident status. Once the conditional basis was removed and they became full-fledged LPRs, these restrictions would no longer have applied and they would have been eligible for grants. By contrast, under the House-approved version of the DREAM Act and the various Senate bills, aliens who obtained full-fledged LPR status would have remained ineligible for grants.

H.R. 6327

The Citizenship and Service Act of 2010 (H.R. 6327), introduced by Representative Djou, was similar to H.R. 1751 in many respects but noticeably different than that bill in others. Like some other DREAM Act bills but unlike H.R. 1751, H.R. 6327 would not have repealed IIRIRA §505. In addition, unlike all the other DREAM Act bills in the 111th Congress discussed here, H.R. 6327 would have required eligible aliens to serve in the uniformed services for at least two years in order to become full-fledged LPRs. Higher education would not have been an alternative to this service requirement under H.R. 6327.

Like H.R. 1751, H.R. 6327 would have enabled eligible unauthorized students to adjust to LPR status in the United States through the cancellation of removal procedure. Aliens could have applied for cancellation of removal without first being placed in removal proceedings, and there would have been no limit on the number of aliens who could be granted cancellation of removal/adjustment of status.

To be eligible for cancellation of removal/adjustment of status under H.R. 6327, an alien would have had to demonstrate that he or she had been physically present in the United States for a continuous period of not less than five years immediately preceding the date of enactment, had not yet reached age 16 at the time of initial entry, and had been a person of good moral character since the time of application. The alien also would have had to demonstrate that he or she had been admitted to an institution of higher education in the United States, or had earned a high school diploma or the equivalent in the United States.

As under H.R. 1751, an alien applying for cancellation of removal/adjustment of status under H.R. 6327 would have had to demonstrate that he or she was not inadmissible or deportable on INA criminal, security, or smuggling grounds. Also like H.R. 1751, H.R. 6327 provided for expedited processing of applications without an additional fee.

Aliens granted cancellation of removal under H.R. 6327, as under H.R. 1751, would have been adjusted initially to conditional permanent resident status. Such conditional status would have been valid for six years and would have been subject to termination. The time an alien spent as a conditional LPR would have counted for naturalization purposes, but the conditional basis would have had to be removed before the alien could apply to naturalize.

To have the condition removed and become a full-fledged LPR, an alien would have had to apply during a specified period and meet additional requirements. Among these requirements, the alien would have had to have demonstrated good moral character during the period of conditional permanent residence; could not have abandoned his or her U.S. residence; and would need to have served in the uniformed services for at least two years. Unlike the other DREAM Act bills in the 111th Congress, H.R. 6327 would not have offered conditional residents the option of completing at least two years of higher education as an alternative to serving in the uniformed services.

H.R. 6327, like H.R. 1751, would have placed temporary restrictions on the eligibility of aliens who adjusted to LPR status under its provisions for federal student financial aid under Title IV of the Higher Education Act of 1965, as amended. Aliens adjusting status under the bill would have been ineligible for federal Pell Grants and federal supplemental educational opportunity grants while in conditional permanent resident status. Once the conditional basis was removed and they became full-fledged LPRs, these restrictions would no longer have applied.

S. 729 and S. 3827

S. 729, the DREAM Act of 2009, and S. 3827, the DREAM Act of 2010, were highly similar bills introduced by Senator Durbin. Differences between S. 729 and S. 3827, as discussed below, concerned the applicable grounds of inadmissibility and the application process under the bills.

Both S. 729 and S. 3827 would have repealed IIRIRA §505 and thereby eliminated the restriction on state provision of postsecondary educational benefits to unauthorized aliens. They also would have enabled eligible unauthorized students to adjust to LPR status in the United States through cancellation of removal. S. 729 and S. 3827 would have enabled aliens to affirmatively apply for cancellation of removal without first being placed in removal proceedings, and they would have placed no limit on the number of aliens who could be granted cancellation of removal/adjustment of status.

To be eligible for cancellation of removal/adjustment of status under S. 729 and S. 3827, an alien would have had to demonstrate that he or she had been physically present in the United States for a continuous period of not less than five years immediately preceding the date of enactment of the act; had not yet reached age 16 at the time of initial entry; had been a person of good moral character since the time of application; and had not yet reached age 35 on the date of enactment. The alien also would have had to demonstrate that he or she had been admitted to an institution of higher education in the United States, or had earned a high school diploma or the equivalent in the United States.

Under both bills, the alien could not have been inadmissible on INA criminal, security, smuggling, or international child abduction grounds and could not have been deportable on INA criminal, security, or smuggling grounds; S. 3827 also would have made applicable the INA ground of inadmissibility barring practicing polygamists. In addition, under both bills, the alien would have had to show that he or she had never been under a final administrative or judicial order of exclusion, deportation, or removal, with some exceptions.

S. 729 and S. 3827 included some different language concerning the application process. S. 729 included a provision, not included in S. 3827, to consider applications on an expedited basis without charging an additional fee. S. 3827 included a provision, not included in S. 729, establishing a deadline for submitting initial cancellation of removal/adjustment of status applications.

Aliens granted cancellation of removal under S. 729 or S. 3827 would have been adjusted initially to conditional permanent resident status. Such conditional status would have been valid for six years and would have been subject to termination. To have the condition removed and become a full-fledged LPR, an alien would have had to submit an application during a specified period and meet additional requirements. Among these requirements, the alien would have needed to have demonstrated good moral character during the period of conditional permanent residence; could not have abandoned his or her U.S. residence; and would have needed either to have earned a degree from an institution of higher education (or to have completed at least two years in a bachelor's or higher degree program) in the United States, or to have served in the uniformed services for at least two years.

The time an alien spent as a conditional LPR would have counted for naturalization purposes under S. 729 and S. 3827. Typically, an alien must be in LPR status for five years before he or she can naturalize. Under both bills, however, the condition on the LPR status would have to have been removed before an alien could apply for naturalization.

S. 729 and S. 3827 would have placed restrictions on the eligibility of aliens who adjusted to LPR status under their provisions for federal student financial aid under Title IV of the Higher Education Act of 1965, as amended. Aliens adjusting status under S. 729 or S. 3827 would have been eligible only for student loans, federal work-study programs, and services (such as counseling, tutorial services, and mentoring), subject to the applicable requirements. Unlike other LPRs, they would have been ineligible for federal Pell Grants or federal supplemental educational opportunity grants.

S. 3962 and S. 3963

S. 3962 and S. 3963 were two highly similar versions of the DREAM Act of 2010, introduced by Senator Durbin in the 111th Congress. They were also similar to S. 3827, another version of the DREAM Act of 2010, which is discussed above. The main difference between S. 3962 and S. 3963 on the one hand and S. 3827 on the other was that the former bills would not have repealed IIRIRA §505 and thus would not have eliminated the statutory restriction on state provision of postsecondary educational benefits to unauthorized aliens. As discussed below, S. 3962 and S. 3963 differed from one another with respect to the cutoff age for eligibility for cancellation of removal/adjustment of status.

S. 3962 and S. 3963 would have enabled eligible unauthorized students to adjust to LPR status in the United States through cancellation of removal. Both bills would have enabled aliens to affirmatively apply for cancellation of removal without first being placed in removal proceedings, and they would have placed no limit on the number of aliens who could be granted cancellation of removal/ adjustment of status. There would have been a deadline for submitting initial cancellation of removal/ adjustment of status applications.

To be eligible for cancellation of removal/adjustment of status under S. 3962 and S. 3963, an alien would have had to demonstrate that he or she had been physically present in the United States for a continuous period of not less than five years immediately preceding the date of enactment of the act, had not yet reached age 16 at the time of initial entry, and had been a person of good moral character since the time of application. Both bills also included an eligibility requirement concerning the age of the alien on the date of enactment of the legislation. Under S. 3962, the alien would have had to demonstrate that he or she had not yet reached age 35 on the date of enactment. Under S. 3963, the alien would have had to demonstrate that he or she had not yet reached age 30 on the date of enactment. Under both bills, the alien also would have had to demonstrate that he or she had been admitted to an institution of higher education in the United States, or had earned a high school diploma or the equivalent in the United States.

As under S. 3827, an alien applying for relief under S. 3962 and S. 3963 would have had to show that he or she was not inadmissible on INA criminal, security, smuggling, polygamy, or international child abduction grounds, and was not deportable on INA criminal, security, or smuggling grounds. The alien also would have had to show that he or she had never been under a final administrative or judicial order of exclusion, deportation, or removal, with some exceptions.

Aliens granted cancellation of removal under S. 3962 or S. 3963 would have been adjusted initially to conditional permanent resident status. Such conditional status would have been valid for six years and would have been subject to termination. The time an alien spent as a conditional LPR would have counted for naturalization purposes, but the conditional basis would have had to be removed before the alien could apply to naturalize.

To have the condition removed and become a full-fledged LPR, an alien would have had to submit an application during a specified period and meet additional requirements. Among these requirements, the alien would have needed to have demonstrated good moral character during the period of conditional permanent residence; could not have abandoned his or her U.S. residence; and would have needed either to have earned a degree from an institution of higher education (or to have completed at least two years in a bachelor's or higher degree program) in the United States, or to have served in the uniformed services for at least two years.

S. 3962 and S. 3963 would have placed restrictions on the eligibility of aliens who adjusted to LPR status under their provisions for federal student financial aid under Title IV of the Higher Education Act of 1965, as amended. Under that act, LPRs and certain other eligible noncitizens may receive federal student financial aid. Aliens adjusting status under S. 3962 or S. 3963, however, would have been eligible only for student loans, federal work-study programs, and services (such as counseling, tutorial services, and mentoring), subject to the applicable requirements. Unlike other LPRs, they would not have been eligible for federal Pell Grants or federal supplemental educational opportunity grants.

S. 3992

S. 3992, another version of the DREAM Act of 2010 introduced by Senator Durbin, would, like the other DREAM Act bills in the 111th Congress, have enabled eligible unauthorized students to adjust to LPR status in the United States. Its legalization provisions were similar to those in the House-approved DREAM Act amendment to H.R. 5281, although there were some differences between the measures, as discussed below. Also like the House-approved amendment, S. 3992 would not have repealed IIRIRA §505 and thus would not have eliminated the statutory restriction on state provision of postsecondary educational benefits to unauthorized aliens.

Under S. 3992, as under the House-approved DREAM Act amendment to H.R. 5281, an eligible alien could have gone though the cancellation of removal procedure and been granted conditional *nonimmigrant* status. An alien could have affirmatively applied for cancellation of removal without first being placed in removal proceedings, and there would have been a deadline for submitting initial cancellation of removal applications. There would have been no limit on the number of aliens who could be granted cancellation of removal under S. 3992.

To be eligible for cancellation of removal/conditional nonimmigrant status under S. 3992, an alien would have had to meet requirements similar to those in the House-approved version of the DREAM Act. The alien would have had to demonstrate that he or she had been physically present in the United States for a continuous period of not less than five years immediately preceding the date of enactment of the legislation, had not yet reached age 16 at the time of initial entry, had been a person of good moral character since the date of initial entry, and was younger than age 30 on the date of enactment. The alien also would have had to demonstrate that he or she had been admitted to an institution of higher education in the United States, or had earned a high school diploma or the equivalent in the United States, and that he or she had never been under a final administrative or judicial order of exclusion, deportation, or removal, with some exceptions. Unlike under the House-approved DREAM Act amendment to H.R. 5281, there would have been no surcharges on applications under S. 3992.

The same grounds of inadmissibility and deportability would have applied under S. 3992 as under the House-approved DREAM Act language. An alien applying for relief under this bill would have had to show that he or she was not inadmissible on INA health-related, criminal, security, public charge, smuggling, student visa abuse, citizenship ineligibility, polygamy, international child abduction, or unlawful voting grounds, and was not deportable on INA criminal, security, smuggling, marriage fraud, public charge, or unlawful voting grounds.[45] Applicants would further have needed to satisfy requirements concerning convictions for offenses under federal or state law; submit biometric and biographic data, which would have been used to conduct background checks; and register under the Military Selective Service Act, if applicable.

Aliens whose removal was cancelled under S. 3992 would have been granted conditional nonimmigrant status. Such conditional status would have been valid for 10 years (compared to H.R. 5281's initial period of five years, which could have been extended for a second five-year period) and would have been subject to termination.

For adjustment to LPR status, the conditional nonimmigrant would have had to submit an application during a specified period and meet requirements similar to those in other DREAM Act bills. Among these requirements, the alien would have needed to have demonstrated good moral character during the period of conditional nonimmigrant status; could not have abandoned his or her U.S. residence; and would have needed either to have earned a degree from an institution of higher education (or to have completed at least two years in a bachelor's or higher degree program) in the United States, or to have served in the Armed Forces for at least two years. Other requirements included satisfaction of the English language and civic requirements for naturalization, payment of federal taxes, submission of biometric and biographic data, and completion of background checks. There would have been no limitation on the number of individuals eligible for adjustment of status under S. 3992.

Aliens who adjusted status under S. 3992 and met other requirements would have been eligible for naturalization after three years in LPR status. The time spent in conditional status under S. 3992, as under the House-approved DREAM Act amendment to H.R. 5281 (during which the aliens would have been conditional nonimmigrants as opposed to conditional LPRs under the other DREAM Act bills), would not have counted for naturalization purposes.

---

[45] The Secretary of Homeland Security would have the authority to waive some of these grounds for humanitarian, family unity, or public interest purposes.

Like the House-approved DREAM Act amendment to H.R. 5281, S. 3992 would have placed restrictions on the eligibility of aliens who adjusted status under its provisions for federal student financial aid under Title IV of the Higher Education Act of 1965, as amended. Aliens granted conditional nonimmigrant status or LPR status under S. 3992 would have been eligible for student loans, federal work-study programs, and services (such as counseling, tutorial services, and mentoring), subject to the applicable requirements. Unlike other LPRs, they would not have been eligible for federal Pell Grants or federal supplemental educational opportunity grants.

S. 3992 also contained provisions like those in the House-approved DREAM Act amendment to H.R. 5281 on the treatment for other purposes of aliens who were granted conditional nonimmigrant status or LPR status under the bill. It provided that conditional nonimmigrants would have been considered lawfully present for all purposes except for provisions in the Patient Protection and Affordable Care Act (PPACA), as enacted by the 111th Congress,[46] concerning premium tax credits and cost sharing subsidies.[47] It also provided that aliens who adjusted to LPR status under the bill would have been deemed to have completed the five-year period required for LPR eligibility for certain types of federal public assistance, as established by the Personal Responsibility and Work Opportunity Reconciliation Act (PWORA) of 1996.[48]

Author Contact Information

Andorra Bruno
Specialist in Immigration Policy
abruno@crs.loc.gov, 7-7865

---

[46] P.L. 111-148, March 23, 2010.

[47] For information on the PPACA provisions, see CRS Report R41714, *Treatment of Noncitizens Under the Patient Protection and Affordable Care Act.*

[48] For information on current eligibility policy, see CRS Report RL33809, *Noncitizen Eligibility for Federal Public Assistance Policy Overview and Trends.*

www.ingramcontent.com/pod-product-compliance
Lightning Source LLC
Chambersburg PA
CBHW081416170526
45166CB00010B/3369